MAMUDAH
THE GREAT ONE!

Written by T. Benton-Parker

This Book is Dedicated to Victor
- *My Love, The Ultimate Football Fan*
&
Billy and Elijah
- *May Your Strong,
Yet Humble Spirits Live On*

Once there was a father who had two sons.

The oldest son's name was William.
He was tall and handsome just like his father.

The younger son's name was Mamudah. He was not as tall or handsome as his brother or father. He was just a plain simple boy, but he was smart and loved to read.

Mamudah loved to read about sports. His favorite sport was football. Quarterback was his favorite position. Mamudah knew the quarterback gets a lot of attention and is often the star of the team. He also knew that in order to be a quarterback, he must spend time studying playbooks.

Mamudah was never allowed to tag along to have fun with his father and brother.

Every time he was by himself, he would study.

He studied things he learned at school. But most of all, he studied his favorite sport—football.

After spending the day together, his father and brother usually returned home at dinnertime. Mamudah had to have everything prepared and ready for dinner. He would set the table, clean the kitchen, and wash the dishes.

Once everyone was finished eating, he would carry a huge pail of trash to the end of the street.

After all of his chores were complete, it was time for bed. He made sure everything was ready for school the next morning.

In the mornings, the boys walked to school together. William would always walk faster, so that he could leave Mamudah behind.

Although the boys went to the same school, no one knew that they were brothers. William was very popular and the other students treated him as if he was a school hero. His brother on the other hand, was hardly noticed.

While at lunch, William sat with all of his popular friends, but poor old Mamudah sat all alone.

Because William was so popular,
the smart kids did his homework for him.

They carried his books and treated him special.

However, his brother never had anyone
to do his work for him. Mamudah was
very smart and he was a hard worker.

One day after school, while the boys were heading home, Mamudah noticed a sign posted:

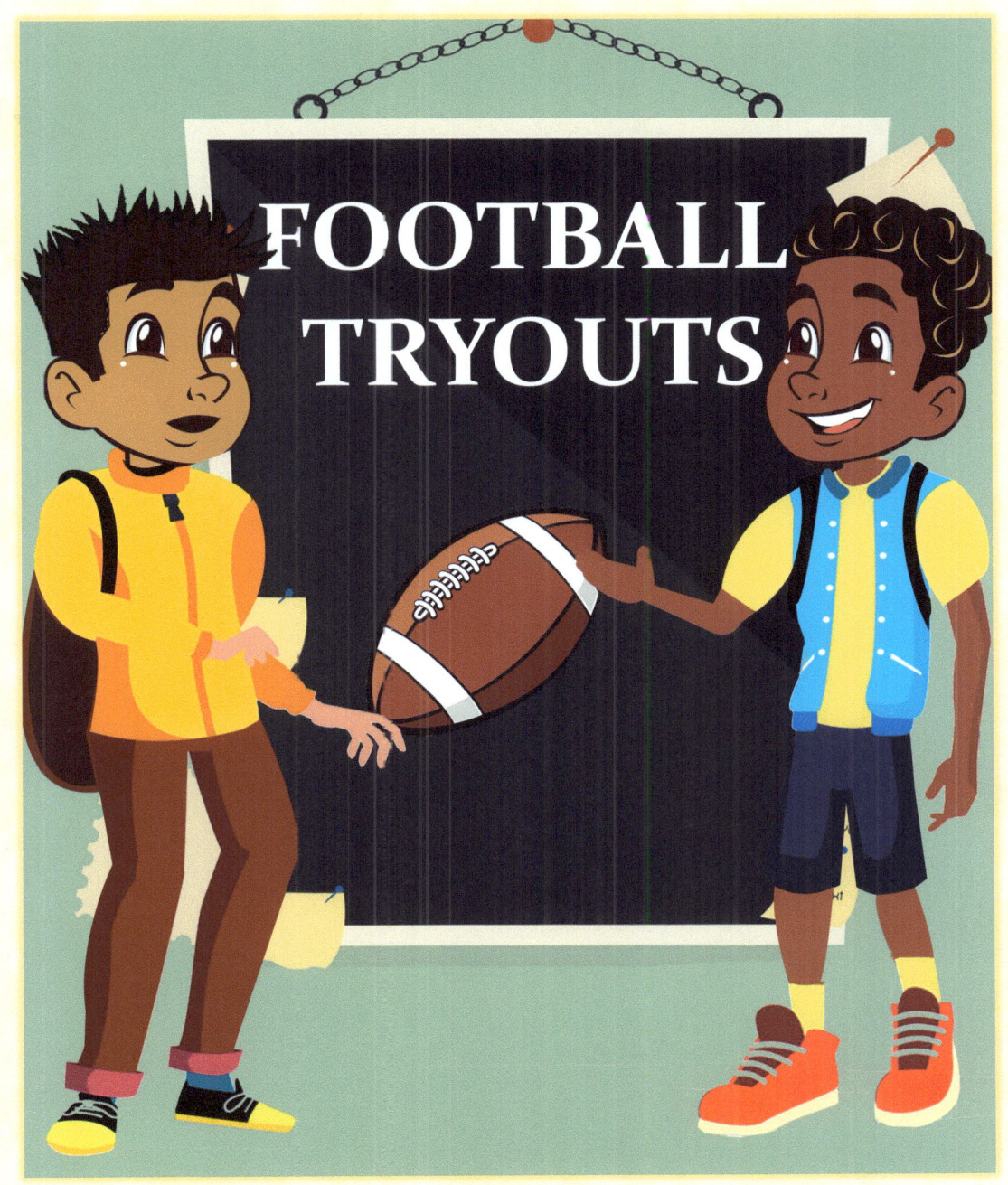

Mamudah shuttered in amazement.
He turned to his brother William and said,
"Will you stay after school with me tomorrow?
I'm going to tryout for football!"
William replied,
"Sure, I will stay, but you will not make the team."

That night when the boys got home,
        Mamudah started doing his chores right away.
    He set the table,
            washed the dishes,
                            and carried that huge
                            pail of trash to the
                            end of the street.

After he finished, he headed straight to bed.
    While he slept, he dreamt about making the team.

The next day when the boys arrived at school, Mamudah reminded William, "Please don't forget about football tryouts today."

William replied, "I won't ! Just don't tell anyone you're my brother. I don't want you to embarrass me."

As soon as school was over,
Mamudah raced to the football field.

There were others waiting to tryout too.

William and his friends sat in the bleachers waiting to watch the players tryout.

To William's surprise, Mamudah was one of the best players on the field. Wow! All those days of carrying that heavy pail of trash to the corner paid off. Mamudah was very strong. He could run fast, score touchdowns, and tackle other players.

Mamudah's dream had come true! He was the best player on the field. He was awarded the position of running back. The primary role of the running back is to block, receive handoffs from the quarterback for rushing plays, and to line up as a receiver to catch the ball in the backfield.

Finally, after many days of practicing, the team was ready for their first game. The whole school was watching. Their opponents were big. Mamudah was a little anxious but he was confident in the sport he loved. The play was called. The quarterback was in position and threw the ball toward Mamudah.

Mamudah caught the ball and ran it into the end zone for the first touchdown. Time after time he scored. At half time, his team was in the lead. At the end of the 4th quarter, they won the game. The whole school cheered. The final score was 28 to 46. Mamudah was the most valuable player of the game.

The next day at school, the other students were so proud of Mamudah. This was the first time they won against their rival team.

It was a great day for Mamudah because this time he was not sitting alone in the lunchroom.

He sat with the popular kids.

Instead of everyone treating William like the school hero, they now treated Mamudah as if he was the school hero.

Game after game, Mamudah scored great!
He made touchdown after touchdown
and led his team to victory.

Meanwhile, William was not as popular anymore
so the cheerleaders stopped doing his homework.

Mamudah saw William after school one day with a gloomy face.

William was saddened because he failed a class.

Mamudah told him not to worry because he would help him. For the first time ever, William smiled at Mamudah and said, "I am thankful you are my brother."

After Mamudah graduated high school, he attended Grambling State University (GSU) in Louisiana.

GSU is an historical university. It was the home of the first African American quarterback to win the Super Bowl, Doug Williams, who had went on to play for the Tampa Bay Buccaneers.

GSU is also the home of the legendary coach, Eddie Robinson. Football experts say he is one of the greatest coaches in history. He has the third most victories in college football history. Eddie Robinson was inducted into the Football Hall of Fame in 1997.

After Mamudah graduated from college, he went on to play for the Miami Dolphins in sunny Florida. The Miami Dolphins were once the home of Dan Marino, the number one NFL draft pick in 1983. Dan Marino was Mamudah's favorite player of all time!

Although Mamudah lives in another state, he still visits his brother William and his father. The three of them sit around the table eating and talking about football. Mamudah's father shared a story about his grandfather. He said that his grandfather was a brave leader in his country. He told Mamudah that he was named after his grandfather.

"Your name," he explained, "means great one."

William and his father both agreed that Mamudah's strong, yet humble spirit was worthy of this great name.

About the Author

T. Benton-Parker lives in Viera, Florida where she has been a teacher for more than 21 years. She realized the stories she had written and told decades ago could come to life in books when an author friend, she calls little Kellie, planted a seed of encouragement. It was also prophesied by her pastors, Dr. R. Shaun Ferguson and Rick Banks that she would write several books.

She owes creating her stories to her children (Shantae, Tamera, Joseph, Marcus, and Aundrey) because they were her captive audience. Her oldest sister Raina, also encouraged her to write as a young girl.

In addition to writing teacher and children's stories, she sings, writes lyrics, and performs in the community theater.

Mamudah The Great One! was created with a boy named Mamudah in mind. He too, was a high school football player with a humble spirit.

T. Benton-Parker can be contacted by email:

benton.parker@gmail.com

Mission: To Proclaim Transformation and Truth

Published by: Transformed Publishing
Website: www.transformedpublishing.com
Email: transformedpublishing@gmail.com

Copyright © 2021 by T. Benton-Parker

Illustrations purchased by T. Benton-Parker from a third party freelance illustrator

Permission to use the names of Mamudah and Doug Williams was granted to T. Benton-Parker

Information stated about Grambling State University, Eddie Robinson, and Dan Marino (Miami Dolphins) was retrieved from https://www.gram.edu/aboutus/ on 1/22/21 and https://www.profootballhof.com/players/dan-marino/biography/ on 1/22/21

All rights reserved solely by the author. No part of this book may be reproduced, stored in a retrieval system, or transmitted in any form or by any means without expressed written permission of the author.

ISBN: 978-1-953241-08-5
Printed in the U.S.A.

www.ingramcontent.com/pod-product-compliance
Lightning Source LLC
Chambersburg PA
CBHW041100070526
44579CB00002B/29